A POETRY BOOK

BY

NAUSICAA TWILA

FOR THE STARS OF MY LIFE

$R + A$

FARAWAY LANDS

Once, those visions of faraway lands were enough to soothe my aching heart. Now, I must reach further into my imagination, for shores that wipe clean the cracks in my bones and skies that are painted with wisdom. I have reached the border of my own creation, where dreams call for me to leave the weights of who I thought I should be. My mind is made up of riddles and mazes that fall away when I remember that I created them.

T E C H N I C O L O R   D R E A M ~ S C A P E

When I wake up from this technicolor dream~scape, I hope you will be holding my head in your lap, telling me it is alright, and that you will remain with me even when I am black and white.

FOREIGNER

I don't fit in because I am changeable,
restless, a dreamer. I watch the sky for answers.
I seek messages from the angels. Who does
that? I do. Because, it seems, I am waiting for
something to happen. something great to shake
me up and take me home. But, it hasn't arrived
yet. So, I watch and wait and pray that I survive
these strange conditions with my adaptability
and resourcefulness to keep me sane.

T H O S E   N I G H T S

Everything was chaos and wilderness, but,
those nights, remember those nights? It would
be so dark, but a stream of light would break
through our hearts. We would laugh like
children, we would chase the sky. Remember?
We would slip out of our bodies and clasp each
other by the soul, and become more than
invincible. Those memories keep me alive.
Some nights, I tell myself that I am the same
one who felt those things, and I feel them again.
No one can touch me there. *Just souls.* And, for a
moment, *I remember who I really am.*

O P E N   A I R

i am tired and hurting and bare--
      i dream of a home in the open air;
and when i dream,
      my eyes sealed shut,
      my home in the distance,
      this little hut...
i dropped the world,
      it was too hard to hold!
      i reached for a sight
      ancient and old...
i am fallen and broken and scared,
      i go my home,
      where i can be bare...

MORE ALIVE

I didn't know what to do with myself once the pain ended. I knew who I had been, but no longer knew who I was. It is true that the pain had changed me, but the question remained, how? *How had I changed?* Was I more ruthless, more alive, stronger, wiser? The truth is that I didn't actually know. And this not knowing burned a hole through me that haunted me for many days and nights, until I woke up from this turmoil, renewed. I didn't know who I was; life was renewed. I finally had my second chance. And I was, indeed, *more alive...stronger...wiser...and, more ruthless.*

INVISIBLE HELPERS

None of this is real. It's a construct. Life is
made up of what we construct. You can start
today. You are free to continue or discontinue
anything you have built thus far. Today, you can
lay down a foundation for anything you can
dream up. The work you put in is only part of
what makes it evolve and breathe. The other
parts are unseen, and unknowable. Call them
"invisible helpers". But, you are still building the
skeleton of this creation. You create the basic
structure. All else is left up to the magic of
natural evolution.

U N D E R G R O U N D   S P A R K

I have no precious keepsakes in my
pockets. I have lost enough to drive me mad.
Instead, it has driven me deeper underground. I
built a home there, where I need nothing except
my own spark to keep me warm, sane and
present.

S E L F   W O R T H

They said a million things into the back pockets
of your dreams. Or maybe they said nothing,
looked away, stared blankly. Maybe they gave
you a feeling that stayed with you all this time.
Something like, *"Oh yeah? You are nothing much to
me or anyone."* You wrestled with this feeling for
many days and nights, to overcome it, to prove
it wrong, always coming up empty handed. Only
later did you learn that you can't prove anything
to anyone who doesn't want to believe. So you
learned to believe in yourself which silenced
their voices and gave dawn to a new era which
you called *"Self Worth"*.

HALF WAY TO NOWHERE

I'm always half-way to nowhere. When they tell you it's better to jump in with both feet, I will say, *look before you leap.* The regrets I have are not about holding back but going full force. At the same time, *I can't regret.* It was a hard climb but I keep on going up. I don't regret not biting my tongue, telling of all the muddy footprints you left on my soul. If it was me, I would have apologized and moved on. I have no pet peeves, but if I did, it would be the excuses and denials that keep on falling from your mouth. Do these eyes look like they don't see right through you? Anyhow, I forgive. Just don't step on the scars you left a second time. *I won't be the silent holder of injustice again.*

I T ' S   A L R I G H T

How do I feel tonight?
I feel bottomless and empty and bare, like each breath
takes conscious effort, buried under blankets and trying
to forget. I have locked my doors and sealed my inner
floodgates shut. I can't imagine how life would be without
these tidal waves but I know this much: I am the ocean.
I breathe deep blue and exhale storms.
It's alright,
it's alright,
it's alright.

FORGET ME SONG

and i will let it go,
and i will let it bleed
         (underneath the cracked sides of my insides)
you see, there is always hope,
around and in between
         (the last days of our ever tides)
inside i will scream things like
         "how could you?"
all while mouthing the words
         "it's OK"
because i know this pain is only partly mine
don't mind me i can take it
it's futile anyway
to repeat the words
you barely even remember
so I will forget them too.
                  (forget them too...)

G O   H O M E

Just put it all away;
All your ambitions,
All you've ever wanted to be.
All you were sure you would be.
All you desperately wanted to be.

Yes, have dreams.
But don't let them have you.

Pick up that which you want to do,
and only that.
Simplify.
Go home.

WINGS ABLAZE

If I could, I would, and let's just leave it at that, shall we? I know it makes you feel important to put dreamers like me in their place, while those around you overlook all your fumblings, but, look—I have gone down this road too many times to lay here silently. I am not just a phoenix rising from ashes, I have flown with wings ablaze for many more miles than you've walked barefoot on clouds. Let me fly by or be burned by these wings. I am a dreamer with a powerful vision beyond your peripheral vision.

YOU ARE NEVER ALONE

Be ready for a fight.

They will try to pin their lack of integrity on
your trusting nature. They will try to make you
fall apart. They want you to look crazy. People
will support you in silence. You must stand on
your own.

But, hear this: *you are never alone.*

You have your voice. You have invisible
helpers. You have the odds on your side. And,
you have allies. When seeking someone to trust
remember this: you are not the first one they did
this to. Cross over to the other side. You will
find the help you need in those who already
fought these battles.

FREE + HONEST

My child, there is no tip toeing around it; *so much of this world is savage.* We live simultaneously in right doings and wrong doings. Justification dances with Justice. There is no escaping the gray areas of life. My child, I will do my best to show you how to laugh and play, even in the gray. I will teach you, above all, to follow your deepest heart, and be free and honest, *despite it all.*

FOR   GOOD

When you crept to my window
and ignored the keep out signs yet again, I wasn't filled
with the terror you normally provoke. That's when I
realized I had already stolen my soul back, and the ghost
at my window was just a reflection of my greatest fear
leaving me for good.

CONFESSIONS, REMINDERS, MISTAKES

How many more breaths can I take? How long until it's over? When will this pass? What is a life that holds a grudge against its very own soul?

I ask myself these things every time I trip, every time I fall, every time my belongings land around me chaotically, every time the door won't close just right. It pops out of its socket and this bothers me more than it makes logical sense to. I am always consciously thinking "step, step, step..." when I walk. Some will call that meditation, but I know it's a compulsion. I keep having to remind myself to wiggle out of mistakes, repeat things that are good for me, and resist the urge to burn progress to the ground.

I think: *"breathe in, breathe out. Smile to that stranger. Help him or her. Be your best..."*

I don't know how to simply *"be"*.
Or maybe That is simply *me, being.*

EXISTENTIAL FREEDOMS

There are some of us not meant for the public eye. We do not thrive under all consuming gazes. We live beyond the image of things. But, we still wish to be heard. We still wish to be seen. We still wish to be loved. We live outside of the world and our purpose is finding peace with that.

RELATIVE WHOLENESS

The world has turned in on itself again and
the sky is a shade of purple I don't understand. I
have hunches and relative wholeness, but inside,
I am separated and bare. The dreams have
passed me, *I am on the edge of the universe.*

A DIRTY TRICK

It's a trick, you see, a dirty trick that life will play. It will say, *"Come on, just a little further, just a little more to do, and then, you will be happy."* And you will run off, out of breath, with your arms full, chasing some savage wish for a better life. But, be very careful, *Bright One*, because life is many things, and among those things, she is a trickster. She will tell you every time, that you must pay for later with your nows. And I will tell you only this: throw all you want into the wind but never your nows. Cherish them always, for *that is the real secret to happiness.*

I UNDERSTAND

We wear our hearts on our sleeves as
badges of loyalty and honor. We get off at train
stations, expecting those we left with to join us.
But, you see, our journey is much longer and
deeper than most. Most get off at the first stop
and we are left alone searching for another soul
who understands.

My friend, I understand.

WILD IMPRISONED

For the wild imprisoned.

Who, in the darkest hour of night, emerge,
under a ruthless moon. Who, hold keys in
sweaty palms, clenched with fear. Fear of what?
Fear of freedom. *Where shall we go? Where is home?*

For timid feet upon foreign grounds.

Break free, *break free wild soul!*
The cage is gone, the fear is gone—

                    only freedom remains.

WORTH THE EFFORT

Go within often and share a fraction of
what you find there. You don't have to share
everything all the time. Many people won't
understand your inner language and many more
will not care. Only a small percentage will feel it
too, and those are the people worth speaking
your heart to. Sift through everyone to find
them.

They are worth the effort.

LET MAGIC FALL

let
magic fall
into my life
like water flowing
like wind blowing
like secrets kept
like tears unwept
like souls song sung
like life's begun...

let
it be like
some magic will
that bends beautifully
on sacred sills
and lands into
my open arms
let it be so
my will is
done

FERRIS WHEEL

For me, life often feels like a Ferris Wheel. Sometimes, I am on it, enjoying the view, enjoying the ride. Other times, I am dizzy, it is going too fast, it is all too much. Most often, I am simply watching it from the side, waiting for a chance to get on. The longer I wait, the harder it is. Because I start to wonder what it's all about, and who I am, and that maybe, I would just rather go for a walk in the forest instead.

DON'T GROW UP

Don't grow up. That's right; don't do it. Instead, *grow wise.* Instead, *grow playful, grow beautiful, grow inspired.* You see, you cannot control the passing of time. But you *can* control how you use that time. Whether you plant seeds or let the weeds grow out. Whether you focus your mind on beautiful things, or if you let small minds teach you how to think. Don't let them tell you to *"grow up"*...Instead, show them how you are determined to unfold:

WISE, PLAYFUL, BEAUTIFUL INSPIRED.

Then, let them learn from you.

LOOK ON THE WILD SIDE

Take those goggles off, the ones that were placed upon you at birth, when you knew nothing except to gaze deliberately, when those eyes that adored you gave you reasons to smile, now, look with your original eyes.

What do you see?

Those answers that bask right under your nose are yours to claim, yours to do as you will, yours to take your soul back...the wild truth, unfiltered by light or dark, which soaks up the pure beauty of life, that is wild and free and for the sake of itself. *That's where your misplaced freedom got to.*

D O N ' T

And when that deadened feeling takes grip of your throat and tells you to beg for mercy, you just gaze right into its soul and say, *"not today..."* Maybe you have had enough, and maybe you are sick of everything, but, let me tell you something: *right now is not forever.* There are a lot more moments that will grab your heart and soul, fill you with fresh air, new visions, and feelings so beautiful that you cannot yet even comprehend them...

Maybe you don't see it yet, and maybe you are drowning in numbness, but I tell you, it will not last. So, *don't do it;* don't take that moment like it's permanent. There will be more. There is always...

... MORE.

EVERYTHING + NOTHING

They all want you, as decoration, as,
"What will you do for me?" As something...
something to distract themselves. But who comes to
the door when you actually call on them?
Nobody. That's when you learn their wanting was
everything to do with them, and nothing to do with you.

U N C A G E D

It's so strange how we use the word *LOVE*
to cover so many emotions. It shakes itself
loose every time, as if to say,

"YOU CANNOT CAGE ME."

EVERYTHING'S GOING TO BE ALRIGHT

I am in a dark place, *but I am hopeful.*
And, the hopeful part of me travels through my
fingers and writes these words to you. The
future me is reading these words and she smiles.
She confirms to me, with an emotion more
powerful than time, that indeed,

everything's going to be alright.

DIAMOND SOUL

You deserve to be here, don't get it mixed up, you are loved and wanted and all those things you long for. Your presence matters like rain and wind and even more in ineffable ways no words can contain. You are worthy, you are worthy, *you are so very worthy!* Can I say it enough? Can you hear me? *You are precious, Diamond Soul.*

DON'T FORGET IT.

THIS SHIP WILL SAIL AGAIN

It's too painful to think of."
I know that feeling. Frantic, choking, gasping
for air. Anything, anything, *reaching for anything.*
Usually, it's numb pretending. Because while
you cannot think of it, you still feel it. It is too
painful to think of and it is agonizing to feel.
You cannot stop the feeling. It floods you, until
you are a broken ship in a dried up seabed. *What
can happen now?*
The pain will pass.
You will dream again.
The tides will return.
This ship will sail again...

41

BURN

she wanted to set her words on fire,
she wanted to burn with them.
set it all aflame,
blazing, fiery ashes
emotions, inside out,
stark reflections
of premonitions
of all things let go
all things up in flames
and her joy
was a sort of elated madness
that seeped through her eyes
and into all she ever knew.

ENCOUNTER

Meet me on the other side of your false pretenses.
I will be there, *heart in hand and soul revealed.* For
today, let's not be me and you; let's just be
nameless souls wandering this vast landscape,
adoring the adventure before us.

THE GREAT SADNESS

I have a great sadness inside me, but you
don't see it; *clearly you don't.* I have been an
expert at masking it for many years now. I can
cry without tears, I can laugh at the drop of a
hat. But, this great sadness remains, sometimes,
close to the surface, sometimes, deep inside my
underground heart. It is an ocean of humanity's
unexpressed and disowned moods singing itself
to sleep. This great sadness doesn't crush me;

I let it sing.

I let it be.

BREAKING FREE

I'm breaking free, beyond these stars. I'm going all the way, *all the way,* into the dark parts, where the *jewels are,* where the *light breaks,* where the *sea becomes magic* and the shine from our eyes *blinds the pain that once blinded us.*

SPIRAL

Let's spiral back in towards everything we love. Let's find old, forgotten books we once wished to read. *Let's read them now. Le*t's forget grudges. Let's remember timeless moments. let's remember our dreams and carry them with us; life is made up of *that which we carry within.*

DON'T STOP

Just get up and move and *don't stop for anything in the world.* If it matters, *carry it with you,* build your strength, get good at balance. Tell them where you are going, *but don't you stop.* The good ones will run with you or meet you there. The good ones will find you, *even when you are on the move.*

SORRY

I am sorry that life made you cruel.

I am sorry that no one told you it could be
different. When you were a child, I am sorry no
one held you like you mattered. I am sorry you
felt discarded. I am sorry you have been fighting
for so long.

You didn't deserve it.

Maybe it's too late to tell you that there was
never anything wrong with you, just a lot wrong
with the way they treated you.

YOU MATTER

YOU. MATTER. For reasons you are, maybe, still deciphering, or maybe, you know you matter but don't know why. Maybe, you see clues, every day, in the way the sun shines directly on you, or in that warm feeling you get which has no name. *You must know that you matter.* In the quiet moments that feel stolen or in simply the way life keeps on unraveling. You do not need someone to suddenly roll out the red carpet with trumpets and sirens to know your worth. You can keep it deep in your heart as a silent knowing, a quiet confidence that there is no one on this Earth who is quite like you. That unique shine of brilliance that you are is desperately needed in this world. You must know this; *you...matter.*

A W A K E N E D

I drown in my own bones for refuge from the madness that taunts me. In the next moments, a brilliant sun will emerge across the landscape of the question: *"Who am I?"* I won't devour it's fury. Instead, I will take it in my arms and cradle it, like a lost game of my psyche's childhood:

AWAKENED.

OPEN LETTER

Dear City of Life,

Why did you have to tear down my memories?
Why did you flatten my dreams into paved
roads and parking lots? Why did you renovate
my neighborhoods into sleek, florescent malls? I
don't recognize these new soul-less windows,
that wrap around contemporary goals. I blinked,
a thousand years passed, and everything I'd ever
known had forgotten all about me. So I sit in a
swing of the last playground they left
untouched, dreaming of vintage values and a life
that unfolds with the kind of beauty that you
cannot destroy.

OVERHEARD

I overheard a conversation the other day.
He said, "But if you don't let people know you
are lost, how can they help you?" *She said,*
"Because the help I need is found in the eyes of
someone *who sees I am lost,* who stops to notice I
have been gone, or my pace has slowed or my
smile is forced. If they can see those things,
then they will know that I need *caring,* not *help.*"

RUNNING

And we were running;
slamming doors to clubhouses, climbing trees,
and finding our souls in the lostness. When the
stars came and the night shone, we would lie
down in the grass and create universes.
God, I miss us.

ON STRANGE WINDS

Lately, I've got unexplained bruises

In places I'd rather hide.

I've seen much better things than these wasted

And for lesser things I have cried.

But strange aches find me anyway

And they make me swallow my pride.

Because I keep on finding lost blessings

On strange winds and random blue tides.

On strange winds and random blue tides...

TWO OLD WOMEN

Two old women spoke near a mountain stream.
"She left one day, and never returned,"
Said the first one.
"But, where did she go?"
Asked the other.
The first one replied,
"She went home."
The other paused and gazed into the sky.
"I didn't realize she was from another world."
"And neither did she,"
Said the wise one,
"Neither did she..."

LETTER TO MY YOUNGER SELF

There will come a time to choose.

These times will be abundant and it will be *one hundred percent up to you.* The choice may be easy and clear cut or it may be hard, confusing and make you question everything that exists in the world. Sometimes, no matter the path you choose, and how certain you are that you did everything right, *there will still be regret.* The regret won't be anything you did wrong. Regret comes with hard choices, *and that is okay.* Life will twist and turn like that up-sweeping wind you love so much. Your ability to choose is your *gift* and your *anguish.* Just know, that whatever you choose, the words, '*I know you did your best,'* are heaven sent . *Use them often when speaking to yourself.*

GARDENS OF MANY PERSPECTIVES

How do we overcome insidious invisible
lines and silent injustices, blurred into justice?
We reach out to one another. We make friends.
We notice the unnoticed. We look for our
sameness and celebrate our humanity—which
comes differently, in different cultures,
households and backgrounds. It is all beautiful
and we are missing out if we don't seek those
different than us to grow our minds into
gardens of many perspectives.

OCEAN CREATURES

The pond will never be
comfortable for ocean creatures
Wanderers will always seek solace
On the open road
Love is a paradox;
You must let go to hold on.

UNIFY

I worked hard to carry unity in my bones.

The seams tore, I cracked and shattered, pieces
of me scattered, people walked past me without
a clue I was even there. I woke up alone in the
garden of hope, clutching my solitude, accepting
sharp truths of division, and realizing, finally, all
I must unify: *MYSELF.*

OLD PHOTOGRAPH

I came across an old photograph of you;
my heart ached out of my chest. I didn't long for
those times. I did not miss those days. *It was
something else.* It was the passage of time, the
longing to reach out and touch you, the inability
to do so, and the impossibility of that frozen
moment that I was helpless to ... *that's what made
me ache the most.*

HUNGRY BEASTS

They pass through here,
like hungry beasts; chewing up
and spitting out all those in their path.
Fake love, fake compliments and fake truth—
they have mastered—with fake grins
in blistering heat.

TEMPERED DISOBEDIENCE

She looked down slightly, but her eyes still shone with *tempered disobedience.* They knew then, that they would not silence this truth. Not this time. *Not ever again.*

SPIRIT STRIKE

The spirit in me will sometimes go on strike.
It sits stubbornly upon my dreams and wishes.
It refuses to budge. but there is more to the
story. Usually, I am grateful for this strike.
Because that nothing that I did for a while,
saved me from the something that would have
done irreversible damage.

THE MADNESS

I say this to those who
  Create and destroy and
  Travel worlds in between...
Take time away from your craft,
  Do simple things;
Because the madness--
  Oh, the madness!
Loves to creep in--
  And demolish
  All worthy and
  Beautiful wings...

YOU WATCHED ME FALL APART

You watched me fall apart. You saw my scars. You watched the tears fall with my madness. You watched me break and shatter. I saw my many pieces reflected in your eyes. I watched you do nothing. I saw your indifference. I saw you shrug. I saw your indifference, I watched you do nothing! I didn't ask you to be here. You decided to reach out, but then, you neither pulled me into the light nor sat with me in the dark. You simply watched, like I was some spectacle to behold. You watched, did nothing, and for that, I am worse off, than had you just walked by.

SECRET ROOM

I know—I have been gone a long time. But you have to understand, I'm in this controlling relationship with the world, and it doesn't let me get away too much. *Tonight was different.* It was a full moon, so I waited until the world fell asleep. Then, I tip-toed into the secret room of my madness, *where I hide myself.* This room is hidden from the world—it's the place I long to be every minute that I am not. Whenever I go there, *I am me again.* One day, I will leave the world for good, and follow my soul to the realm where freedom *doesn't hide in madness* and wisdom is an unmasked being who *teaches the world to love.*

TOUGH DREAMERS

The toughest souls have the softest hearts and dreams that go on for miles. They have eyes that see more than they tell and minds that paint the world with dreams which open soft hearts of tough dreamers like them.

THE HOMES WE BUILT

I slipped through the cracks of your heart—
I was a void gazing into you; the madness crept in,
as you gazed back. I can barely remember the colors of
those times, and I no longer long for the homes we built.

NO STRINGS

I am not your puppet anymore—
I cut those strings. You see, I was made from
magic material. I don't dance when you say so.
You are not my customer and you are not
always right. I am gathering my hat up, filled
with a few coins. I will walk all night, and I am
not afraid of walking through the dark alone.
Just get me out of this drunken studio with
grabby hands and entitled glares. *My only
endorsement is my own truth.*

LONE WOLVES

Lone wolves
are the strongest.
Remember this, little cub,
when you are feeling
the weakest.

BLAZE SOFTLY

Blaze softly, wild one.
The night is ours and
There is more than right now.
WE LIVE IN FOREVER.

LONGING

After all I've done,
And all I've seen,
And all that's torn me apart—

*I long for
home, most.*

STRANGE THINGS

It is strange to me that people
continue to confuse worth with
image and image with success.

THE ONLY NAME I KNOW YOU BY

I heard you calling
in my dreams, and when
I awoke, I uttered the
only name I know you by:
"HOME..."

MAD WORLD

The world has gone mad,
Let's build a home of our own.

NOTES FROM MY SOUL

I will be there
When the mountains fall
And the summer grows cold
I am your constant
In an ever changing world.

P A R T Y   C R A S H E R S

I believe that the things we never speak out
loud are all together, having a dinner party,
pulling strings, causing drama, magic and
impossible coincidences. I say, crash that dinner
party, *and cause some mischief of your own.*

GATHERING THUNDER

I'm gathering thunder
I'm marking invisible trails
I'm falling down
I'm raising my sails

MY ANCESTORS WERE VIKINGS

Yes, I have a soul who heals,

And loves, and upholds peace;

But, I have warrior's blood in my veins.

I fight forever with Odin's breath in my lungs.

And, when war surrounds me,

I tilt my my head to the sky, and laugh,

Honored to fight alongside ghosts

Who fought for me

Since I was just a dream.

HONEST

You want to be honest?
    Tell me of something
    you've never read before.
    Say what's in your heart,
    be a dream for a moment,
    not anyone else's, but be your
    very own, *real, raw self.*

NOBODY

Hi, I'm nobody.
I hide a well of wisdom
beneath my nothingness.
Only when I am nothing, can
I truly be myself. Mostly, this
will seem like nonsense, but
a few will understand, because
they long to be nobody, too.

CHANGE THE WORLD,
CHANGE YOURSELF

You change the world
by changing the way you
treat everything around you.
*It all starts with the way
you treat yourself.*

SOUL THIEVES

I realize there is no in between with me. I
either feel connection with people, or I don't. I
accept all humans as they are—no judgment.
The defining factor for me, is how they treat
me. I feel the bad vibes immediately, no matter
what they claim. My response is to cut off the
unconditional connection I tried to create. If
they don't want a friend, they likely want to use
me in some way. So, *no thanks*. I am only an
endless resource to true, and loyal friends as
well as lost souls who need a light through their
dark night..*not soul thieves*.

MY NIGHT

I am busy with my night at the moment.

Don't despair if I look gone.

GHOSTS

Sometimes, I think I see you, walking
down streets we once walked down together,
when life was sweet and the world knew my
name. I don't call your name; even if you
answer, it won't be you, just as *I am no longer me.*

ANTIDOTE

I'm different...

Because I will go down that rabbit hole.

With you, alone; it doesn't matter.

And, all I can do, as an antidote,

is reach for rainbows instead.

BACK TO YOU

There is so much wrong
with what you did to
me. Please forgive me,
because I am about to
hand it all back to you.

GIFTED

When they knocked at your door in the wee hours to pronounce the beauty of your wounds, you shot up with new energy, like you had been seen for the first time. The heartache didn't come until you were skin-deep in their praises, made of silk and lilacs; *beautiful, breakable, mortal.* Dried leaves crushed under your feet. You were alone, without morning, without safe zones, but you became your own dawn and weaved safety from ripped fabrics of your own beautiful and wounded heart.

WARRIOR

If I wasn't a warrior,
you would crush me.
But I am a warrior. So
I will save myself and
THIS WILL SAVE YOU TOO.

ATTIC

I have cleaned out
the attic of my
mind many times,
but it remains full
of ancient pictures,
codes I can't decipher
and relics that
mysteriously
make me cry.

FAR FROM NORMAL

Maybe I am far from normal and maybe I don't even know what that is. But I do know this; I am brave and I am loyal and my will is made of battle-ready iron. I am one inch away from being immersed in a life-changing adventure of some kind. So, if you happen find me with my feet on the ground, and my eyes glazed over, that will be me trying hard not to be swept away into another dream, before I can catch my breath.

S E E

No.

You don't understand.

I feel lost and empty with people, except a select few. But,
life separates us, and here we are, alone. I cannot describe
the fullness I feel when I am alone. The skies carry me, I
can fly. I see so many dimensions—too many. You
wouldn't believe me. Only a select few do. Only a select

few,

see, too.

M O R E

No matter how many times
life has thrown me down,
I have overcome, and I know
life has more where that came from.

But, that's OK.

There's also more where I came from.

LOVE YOUR SELF

Love.

Your.

Self.

What does this mean?

It means you see the best in you, and support
your soul to shine as brightly as you can. You
never put yourself down—*ever.* You see the best
in you, and encourage *that.* That is what it
means to

Love

Your.

Self.

STORMY RAINBOWS

And then, it will feel like everyone has forgotten you. That's when life will get really *beautiful*, and really *sad*. That's when the miracles will want to bloom all around you. Be sure to keep your eyes up—*don't miss out on those stormy rainbows.*

BETTER THAN OK

"Are you sure you're OK?"

I heard the words, but they did not register. I had been *KO'ed*—same letters, different order. I was flattened, face to the Earth, wide awake, yet unable to move. Nothing in me felt *"OK"*. I didn't even know how to answer such a question. My mind felt gone and my insides re-arranged.

"I am better than ever."

I heard myself reply. It was honest. I was somehow going to make it so. I was turning my back on every complaint I wanted to make. That was my rebellion. Inside my heart, *flags were burning.*

THE PAIN IS NO LONGER PAIN

Sometimes, the pain is no longer pain; I've sunk beneath it, into a dream. Those moments are special, because what I feel is some sort of bliss. I don't know how, but the anguish of life has transcended. It happened, as if by magic, and it surrounds the tragedy which is my current reality. *Am I coping well with my suffering?* Yes, I would say so. I let go. I found my place beyond the rights and wrongs of the world. *I found my bliss.*

TO HESITATE

And then, *I hesitated.* I don't know why I hesitated. It was not a moment for hesitation, it was a moment for action. But, suddenly, I was painfully uncertain. Imagine that—the universe at my doorstep and I was suddenly *"not sure".* So, the moment passed, *and never returned,* and of course, I dwelt on it for quite some time. It took me many years to learn that sometimes, hesitation is not something to question. It is my compass spinning in all directions. It is OK, and absolutely appropriate—*to hesitate.*

NO BETTER FEELING

I've been getting through.

Hand on my heart, with incredible pressure on
my soul, *I have survived.* It has been heavy, to say
the least. But, once I saw my home on the
horizon, I jogged then ran, then sprinted, then I
kicked my shoes off onto the porch.

I have traveled the world, but right now, there is
no better feeling than coming home.

DARE

Dare yourself to keep going,
in murky waters with no
visible army behind you.

Dare to be brave.
THE MIRACULOUS FOLLOWS THE BRAVE.

TRUST

Our world is based on trust.
You trust the driver in the opposite lane to stay
on his side of the line. You trust the pharmacist
to give you the right dose. You trust the
payment to go through to the right account for
the right price. I have been told I am *too trusting,*
but, aren't we all trusting each other constantly?
"Too trusting" means I do what everyone else
does on a daily basis, only it was used against
me. Now, is it my fault for trusting? *"You should
have read the fine print. You should have asked more
questions. You misunderstood."* Maybe there should
be a law against violating this basic human trust
which we all rely on to survive. Maybe we
should hold people more accountable for
violating this trust, instead of simply saying, *"It
was my fault. I was too trusting."*

UP TO ME

When I shared my pain, and heard you empty response, I realized how alone I truly was. But, I was going to rise without you, with only myself emerging from the deep abyss of my soul. That day, I realized:

IT WAS ONLY UP TO ME.

CANDLEIT DREAMS

Somewhere between
    edge-less wandering and
    organized bliss, I am lost
    with *a book,*
      a candle
        and hope.

SOMEDAYS

Some days,

    You'll find me

    Under some darkened, crazy sky,

    Smuggling truths across my lips,

    Offering freedom a home

        In my wake

DREAMY RESTLESSNESS

It took me a long time to not give a damn
what anyone thought of me. Now that I'm here,
you are welcome to to sit down and share your
opinion. I will smile and say, *"That's interesting,"*
and then I will get back to being the same I've
always been: *dreamy restlessness with a dash of pride.*

L E A R N I N G   T O   E X I S T

Don't touch my healing;
I am still tender from the fall. I said I was fine
and I look fine, but that's just what I need to do
right now. Don't notice my pain, don't correct
me. I am using all my strength to breathe, so,
please, don't turn on the lights just yet.
I am learning to exist all over again.

SO MUCH MORE

You don't have to declare your victim-
hood to be empowered. You can also say:
*"It happened but it was only a moment.
I grew, and I am so much more."*

DEAD ENDS

I cannot stand dead ends. They might be beautiful dead ends, but they are still dead ends. In the same way, conclusions irritate me because they imply there is nothing more. There is always more to discover with our minds and with our hearts. *Why can't we just admit we know less than we pretend to know?*

LONG WALK HOME

Poetry is my long walk home.
It is my sanctuary of nothingness;
No where to get to,
Nothing to do.
It is the promise only I know,
A secret I keep
In my heart's broken room
Bolted shut,
But something magic lives there...
I spit out words on a canvas,
Some beautiful,
Some raw,
All, are welcome.
I spoke to myself many times in dreams,
I said, "Hey, kiddo-- Put down those burdens,
Walk with me a while..."
Poetry is my long walk home
I am walking myself home
And only I know the way...

LOVE, FALTERING, FORGVING

It's true that you hurt me and you can never make up for that pain. But, while dreams were shattered and time stood still, I noticed your golden heart in stolen glimpses as you offered up your share of lost forevers. So I forgave you. That's when this sliver in my heart melted and I could see that we were not so different, you and I; *in love, in faltering, and in forgiving.*

T R A V E L E R

I love to travel.

I have a mind that doesn't sit still, questions everything. It picks everything apart, it over-thinks. I wrestle my mind every day. But, when I travel, everything is new.

I travel so my mind can rest.

MEDICINE FOR MY HEART

I could not find medicine for my heart in any scriptures, in any friend, in any guide; so I began writing my own jagged truths upon the rocks of my existence. Some truths, I found double locked and buried in cement; and they would carry me for miles. Some truths, were like forgotten change in my jean pockets, just barely enough to get me through the night. I cling to my truths, because last night, I was up with terrors and I still have great anguish about my tomorrows. But I keep on uncovering medicine for my soul. And, somehow, *that is everything.*

THANK YOU FOR READING

This book has been a quest to find a permanent home in the impermanence of life. It's been a searching for stability—from the inside out. It's been a quest for fearlessness among the ghosts of the past, and learning to live with *(out)* those ghosts. It's been finding peace in the chaos and allowing my soul to shine. It's been about remembering, while keeping the important memories and discarding the rest. It's been about safe guarding the home of my heart. It's been about learning that I have always been safe.

I wish for you find your home in this mad world, too.

LOVE,

Nausicaa

HOME

NOTES + DREAMS

NOTES + DREAMS

HOME

NOTES + DREAMS

NOTES + DREAMS

HOME

NOTES + DREAMS

NOTES + DREAMS

HOME

NOTES + DREAMS

NOTES + DREAMS

HOME

NOTES + DREAMS

NAUSICAA TWILA

NOTES + DREAMS

Nausicaa Twila is a Canadian Based author and poet who focuses on many subjects of the soul, including the resilience and hope for the human spirit. She has written poetry and writings since childhood, which she became more serious about at 16, when she began journal writing with self-inquiry methods. She is a world traveler, healer and serial over-comer. She is a student and a teacher. She believes anything can be overcome and conquered with focus and intention. She wishes to instill unshakable self-empowerment within herself and others while practicing self-accountability honest and intention. *She is not done yet.*

She has written 9 books of poetry, available on Amazon.com:

1. BEAUTIFUL MINDS ANONYMOUS (A BOOK OF POEMS)
2. BEAUTIFUL MINDS ANONYMOUS II (BURNER OF SHIPS)
3. BEAUTIFUL MINDS ANONYMOUS III (MYTHICAL CREATURES)
4. CHRONICLES FROM ANOTHER REALITY
5. OVERCOMING JOURNAL
6. THE SWEETEST GOODBYE
7. SOLEDAD
8. TAKING MY MAGIC BACK
9. HOME

FIND HER ON FACEBOOK:
Facebook.com/BeautifulMindsAnonymous
OR INSTAGRAM:
Instagram.com/NausicaaTwila
EMAIL:
nausicaatwila@gmail.com

Made in the USA
Lexington, KY
23 March 2018